How to Succeed in a Job Interview

Colvin Tonya Nyakundi

Business and Entrepreneurial Series

JD-Biz Publishing

Check out some of the other Entrepreneur Series books

Entrepreneur Series books on Amazon

Table of Contents

Introduction 4

Preparations before the Interview 6

How to Answer Frequently Asked Questions 12

Apparel and Grooming...16

First Impression and Language Used 19

What to Carry and What Not To Carry 24

Conclusion..27

Author Bio...29

Publisher...40

Introduction

Some people are lucky enough to get several job opportunities in their lifetime. Others are unlucky and get just a few job opportunities. Since you can never be sure of whether you're one of the lucky or unlucky ones, you have to do everything you can to get a good job as soon as an opportunity arises. As soon as there is a vacant position in any firm, an advertisement will be placed on several platforms to invite qualified people to apply to this position. If you applied for the job and were shortlisted as a potential employee, the firm will go ahead and invite you to an interview. The interview will be the single most important determinant of whether you're going to get that job or not.

Throughout the world, companies shortlist several candidates before the best one can be selected to fill a vacant position. This means that you won't be the only person being interviewed for that job. It is up to you to convince the interviewer(s) why they should hire you and not any of the other applicants to that position. You have to be highly distinguishable from all the others.

There are several things that you can do before, during and after the interview so as to increase the probability of getting that job. Some of the factors that might influence whether you'll get the job include your dressing code and grooming, first impression, qualifications and how well you answer questions asked by the interviewer. If you can control all these factors, then you can rest assured that the job is yours. This means that you have to be thoroughly prepared and know what to expect before, during and after the interview.

The book "How to succeed in a Job Interview" is equipped with everything you need to do before, during and after the interview. With the tips listed in this book, you will significantly increase chances of getting that job that you've been dreaming of. Apart from helping you prepare for a job interview, this book will guide you on any other interview including a promotion, admission to college, television interview and even when preparing for an interview after applying for a bank loan.

Start your journey to your dream job by reading the book "How to succeed in a Job Interview."

Preparations before the Interview

An interview is not something that you can just wake up and go to without preparations. If you dare do so, you are most likely not going to get that job. All employers know that you need time to prepare before an interview. That is why they will call you well in advance and schedule an interview at such a time that you will have properly prepared. This way they can be sure that you won't have excuses as to why you can't answer some questions or elaborate further when required to do so.

There are several things that you must do during the preparation stage of an interview. To begin with, you must ensure that you have all the supporting documents to your job application. Such documents include original academic certificates, testimonials and any other document that might help you during the interview. It is also important to make sure that you're qualified for that job. The supporting documents will help you prove that you're qualified for the job.

It is important to note that being qualified doesn't mean that you know the job. This is because some people have the academic credentials but they don't have the experience/expertise to do the job. Before going to any interview, you must ensure that you know how to do the job. After all, you're not being hired so as to gain experience; the company is looking for somebody who can get the job done. If you're just out of college, you can do some research so as to know the job description for professionals in that position. You can also try talking to people occupying that position in other firms so as to know what they do. If you know what you'll be doing if you get hired, the company won't mind giving you the job. You'll also save yourself from the disappointment of doing a job you were not prepared to do or one that you don't like.

Before going for an interview or even applying for any job, you can apply/ request to be an intern in that or any other firm. This way you gain some experience and hence increase chances of getting a job once you start applying for one. Apart from helping you get experience, internship will help you know how to relate with fellow employees in a work environment.

You must know some history about the firm/company you're thinking of working for. During a job interview, it is not uncommon to be asked something about the company. Some of the information that you need to know include the company's products or brands, its subsidiaries, revenues, major achievements, major incidences within the firm, awards etc. You should also know when the company was founded, who founded it, the region it serves and how the company is impacting the local and global community.

While doing research about the company, it is also important to note the organization structure. This basically means that you should know who is in charge of which department. You must know the chief executive officer, chief accountant, human resource manager, head of marketing and any other person in a managerial position within the firm. You also need to know who will be your immediate boss if you get the job.

During the preparation stage, you need to know the exact time and location of the interview. The interview doesn't have to take place within the company's premises. It can take place in some other location including a hotel with a conference room. It will be very unfortunate if you arrive at the company's headquarters/premises only to find out that the interview is supposed to take place elsewhere. Knowing the exact venue of the interview will also help you prepare the logistics of getting there in time. Keep in mind that traffic isn't the same everywhere. The venue of the interview will influence the traffic you'll have to endure before arriving there. The only way that you can reach there in time is if you take into consideration the kind of traffic that is normally experienced there.

Ensure that you've arrived at the job interview venue about 30 minutes before time. This way you can be more prepared before entering the interview room. Arriving in time will also help you not to be nervous or anxious during the interview. Can you imagine what is going to happen if you arrive late and find everybody seated? As soon as you've arrived at the venue, it's important to ensure that you know the exact room where the interview will take place. This way you'll avoid confusion and hence increase chances of getting the job. You should also visit washrooms before entering the interview room.

Never overeat the night before the interview. The last thing you need is a bloated stomach on the day you're being interviewed for a job. Will you request to visit washrooms while you're being interviewed? Supposing you are the interviewer, what impression will you have of an interviewee who is visiting washrooms every few minutes?

You must never drink alcohol when preparing for an interview. Apart from the fact that alcohol impairs judgment, you will create a very bad impression if the interviewer(s) discover that you're drunk. You can also fail to wake up early enough on the date of the interview, if you drunk excessively the previous day. Even if you love drinking alcohol so much, it is of paramount importance that you don't drink on this particular day.

So as to increase chances of getting a job, you should be up to date on new developments in your specialty. This is because the company expects to hire somebody who knows something about technological advancements in his/her field. Since you can be asked any question, you should ensure that you are up to date on current happenings around the world. Recent or trending news on cable television or social media can help you know what is happening currently anywhere in the world. You can be asked anything about politics, education, mining, technological advancements or even the weather.

If you've been invited for a job interview, you have to prepare a simple but detailed resume. A resume is a document that summarizes your qualifications, skills, achievements and personality. Since the resume is a self-advertisement document that will help you sell yourself to the employer, you have to be very careful about how it looks like. It should be formatted properly and contain the relevant information only. Keep in mind that the interviewer doesn't need/want to know all the details about your life. Therefore, you should ensure that the resume contains information that is relevant to the job that you're applying for i.e. it should be brief and straight to the point. You should also ensure that the words used in the resume are not offensive and do not portray you negatively. Information contained in a resume includes bio-data, contact details, academic credentials, hobbies and two or more referees.

When preparing the resume, it is very important to make sure that the information contained is accurate. If you include inaccurate information, the interviewer will just think that you're confused and disorganized. This means that he/she might deny you that job that you've been yearning for. In order to increase chances of getting the job, you have to ensure that all your major achievements have been included in the resume. It's also important to inform your referees that you've included them in your resume. This way a referee won't be caught off-guard in case the interviewer decides to call him/her.

How to Answer Frequently Asked Questions

Regardless of the position you applied for, there are several common questions that you have to be prepared for. These questions are broadly asked throughout the world and help interviewers get to know more details about the candidate. So as to know how to answer such questions, you can try talking to other people who've been interviewed by the same panel before. Below are some of the questions that you should expect to be asked and how to answer them:

- What are your expectations?

When asking this question, the interviewer is trying to figure out the benefits and privileges you're anticipating once you've been hired. If you've been asked this question, you should never be specific by for example stating that you're expecting a fully paid holiday trip to your destination of choice. Just tell the interviewer that you'll be comfortable with the privileges and benefits received by other employees within the company. If you're expecting more than the company can afford, you'll probably not get the job. On the other hand, if you are expecting much, much less than other employees, you might end up being denied what you deserve.

- How much should we pay you?

Interviewers normally ask this question so as to know how much you think you're worth. If you're specific when answering this question, you might end up not getting the job after asking for more than the company can afford to pay you. O the other hand, if you ask for a small salary, you might end up being paid less than what other professionals with your qualifications and experience get paid. Rather than risk being underpaid or not getting the job, you can tell the interviewer that your agent or workers union will negotiate the salary on your behalf. It is also important to make it clear that you're willing to start working with a small salary as long as you're guaranteed of an increase with time i.e. you're willing to grow with the company.

- Can you tell us (me) something about yourself?

That is basically asking about your strengths and weaknesses. You can answer this question by telling the panel something about your hobbies, your family life (are you a husband or dad?) your previous position or anything you think will help you get that job. This question doesn't have any specific answer. You can talk about any aspect of your life; either your personal or professional life. However, you should not be boring or give so much detail especially if you're talking about your personal life. If you decide to talk about your weaknesses, tell the interviewer(s) what you're doing to overcome your weaknesses i.e. how are you countering your weaknesses?

- Why did you leave your past job? Were you fired? Did you resign? Why?

The most important thing when answering this question is that you should never lie. Even if you were fired, you better try to explain why. You should also state what you're doing to avoid doing the same mistake that got you fired. If you resigned from your previous job, just tell the interviewer that you felt you're ready for new challenges. You should never slander or insult your previous employer.

- What makes you different from all the others?

The interviewer asks this question when he/she is trying to find out your strengths i.e. what you're best at. If you're asked this question, you can talk about something extraordinary that you achieved in the past. For instance, you can talk about a situation where you helped expand your previous employer's clientele by coming up with new marketing tactics. You can also talk about how you helped solve a disagreement between two employees working for your previous employer. By talking about such issues, you'll be explaining why you think you're a better leader, a hard-worker and a problem solver.

- Technical questions related to your industry

Apart from personal and general knowledge questions, you should also expect technical questions about your industry. The company is seeking somebody who can do his job, be a leader and a problem solver. For instance, if you're being interviewed for an engineering job, you have to know the technical details about what your company deals in.

- Do you have any questions?

At the end of the interview, the interviewer(s) will want to know if you have any question. This is your opportunity to know what you're about to get yourself into. You have to ask as many questions as you can. However, you should ensure that all your questions are relevant to the job you're being interviewed for. For example you can ask about what you're expected to do or when you're expected to start the job if you get hired etc.

Apparel and Grooming

In any interview, your choice of clothes and grooming will have a huge impact on whether you're going to get that job or not. To begin with perfect choice of clothing and proper grooming will make you confident and hence reduce chances of making mistakes. You'll also create a good impression if you turn up at a job interview well groomed and perfectly dressed. Your choice of clothes and general appearance is even more important if you'll be dealing with clients directly. This means that you have to be very careful about how you dress if you're a banker, customer care agent, marketing executive, human resource manager or work in any other capacity that directly deals with a company's clients. Even if your career deals with machines (e.g. engineering and manufacturing) you still have to look good during the interview.

On the day you're scheduled to be interviewed, you have to shave your beard and trim your hair so as to look presentable i.e. ensure that your hair isn't shaggy and/or dirty. You can also use some hair gel to make your hair more presentable and attractive. However, men should not over apply the gel. That will just make them look more feminine and hence it might affect the probability of getting that job.

Perfume and makeup can also help you look more presentable during an interview. Perfume is quite important if you have bad odors and the interview room is so small that you're very close to the interviewer. Just ensure that you don't over apply makeup or use excessive perfume. When selecting the perfume to use, ensure that it doesn't affect anybody who is hypersensitive to strong smell. Some people are allergic to specific ingredients in perfumes. Can you imagine what is going to happen if your interviewer is allergic to your perfume and then starts sneezing right after you've entered the room? What is the probability that he/she is going to give you that job?

Jewelry can also help ladies look more presentable during an interview. However, you should never wear excessively large jewelry. This will just create a bad impression especially if you're being interviewed for a technical job such as engineering, chemistry or medicine. In such careers, large jewelry is highly discouraged as it increases chances of an accident occurring at the work environment. This means that you might just lose the job if you turn up for an interview with a huge necklace or any other jewelry.

When going for an interview, you should wear official/formal clothing. This means that you must never put on sneakers, boots, jeans, t-shirts or sweatpants. If possible, you should put on a suit and tie. A suit includes a long or short sleeved shirt, blazer and trousers or dress.

Always ensure that the chosen clothes don't make you uncomfortable in any way. You will lose concentration during the interview if you turn up wearing something that makes you uncomfortable. All that you'll be thinking of is when the interviewer will be over so that you can go change to more comfortable pieces of clothes.

You must also ensure that your clothes are not too tight or too sexy. The interviewer will just think that you're trying to flirt with them or manipulate them to give you the job based on your sexuality. Don't put the interviewer in an awkward position; just wear something that is decent and doesn't show too much skin.

First Impression and Language Used

According to scientific research, it takes less than ten seconds to create an impression after meeting somebody for the first time. Within the first ten seconds, somebody can have a rough idea of your personality, character and attitude. Therefore you have to do everything you can to impress your interviewer within the first ten seconds of meeting him/her. Some of the factors that will influence your first impression include your cleanliness and neatness, choice of clothing, posture, gestures, facial expression and choice of words. This means that you have to be very careful about how you look and what you say after meeting the interviewer for the first time.

As soon as you've been ushered into the interview room, you should create rapport between you and the interviewer. A firm handshake that lasts between 3 and 5 seconds can help you create rapport and break the ice after entering the interview room. It's also important that you smile and look happy from the beginning to the end of the interview. A smile will help portray you as a social person who is ready and willing to interact with other people and have a good time at the company's premises. On the other hand, a frown will portray you as a loner and depressed person. If you frown during the entire interview, the interviewer might easily conclude that you won't be able to perform your responsibilities alone or when working as a team.

After entering the interview room, you should not go ahead and sit down. The best thing to do is to wait till the interviewer tells you to sit down. This way you'll portray yourself as a polite and respectful person and hence increase your chances of getting the job. Ensure that you sit in an upright position and face the interviewer directly. You shouldn't open your jacket buttons after sitting down. Opening your jacket buttons create an impression that you're too much relaxed. Don't get too comfortable, you haven't been hired yet.

You must be very organized if you want to be hired for that job. This means that all your documents should be in order and perfectly placed on the table or near you. You should place your documents in such a way that you can easily locate any document within a few seconds.

This way you'll find it easier to substantiate any claims you make by giving the interviewer the relevant documents.

Throughout the interview, it's always important to maintain eye contact with the interviewer. Eye contact will help portray you as a courageous, strong and confident candidate who isn't afraid to do his/her job in front of his/her boss. You must also ensure that your facial expression and gestures match your words and responses. For instance, it is always good to nod while responding with a 'yes'.

During the interview, it is advisable that you listen more and talk less. You should never answer if you haven't understood the question clearly. If necessary, you can seek clarification before answering a question. If you adhere to this principle, you'll create an impression of somebody who can do what he is being told to do. How can you do something if you don't know what you're supposed to do? Seeking clarification will prove that you'll be ready to ask a question if your supervisor is ambiguous or unclear.

Never guess or answer a question if you're not 100 percent sure that you're giving the correct answer. The best way to answer a question is by being honest about everything. If you don't know the answer, you can always tell the interviewer that you will do research so as to find out more information about the issue at hand. This way the interviewer will think of you as a normal person-who doesn't know everything in this world- but is willing and ready to learn something new.

You should never let your emotions control you while in the interview room. Even if you feel the interviewer is making you uncomfortable, try to be calm and answer all questions rationally. All your answers should be based on facts and logic and not on anger or excitement.

As part of the interview process, the interviewer might invite you for lunch or drinks later on in the day or just after coming out of the interview room. Regardless of whether you're at the company cafeteria or in a downtown hotel, you have to be very careful about what you order and how you eat. Even if your interviewer orders beer, you shouldn't order beer or any other alcoholic drink. You should also not overeat or order a meal that is too expensive. Wait till your interviewer has ordered his/her meal then you can order a meal that is within the same price range.

Whether you're asked about it or not, it is never advisable to express or insinuate your religious or political opinion or affiliation. You should also avoid talking about sensitive and ethical issues. Try to portray yourself as a neutral person who is willing to work with anybody regardless of their political affiliation, religion or opinion on sensitive issues.

Cursing words and gestures should never be used in an interview room. Such words show that you're disrespectful and too emotional to handle the job you're being interviewed for. Regardless of what the interviewer said or asked, you should try to be as polite and respectful as possible.

What to Carry and What Not To Carry

If you've been invited for a job interview, you should be prepared how you're going to answer the questions that you will be asked. This means that you must carry everything that will help you answer the questions as accurately as possible. You should be able to substantiate on any claims that you make by using what you have in the interview room. On the other hand, you must avoid carrying unnecessary stuff that will make you look like a hoarder or disorganized person. The best thing to do is carry the necessary stuff and leave out the unnecessary stuff.

You must have your original academic certificates and several copies of the same. Without these crucial documents, you won't be able to prove that you have the required academic qualifications. Apart from academic certificates, you should carry with you a recommendation letter-if you have one- from your previous employer. Copies of your resume should also be availed to your interviewer(s.) After entering the interview room, you should hand over copies of your academic certificates, resume and recommendation letter to each of your interviewers-or at least half of them. This way the interviewer(s) will have something to refer to as you are answering their questions.

It's also important that you bring a long a pen and small notebook. This way you'll be able to write down important points before answering any question. A notebook and pen will also help you become coherent when answering questions. However, you shouldn't start writing anything before seeking permission from the interviewer.

Some companies are very strict when it comes to their employee's health and performance. Such companies include those that deal in food, beverages and pharmaceuticals. When you've been invited to an interview by such companies, you should bring along your medical reports or health clearance certificates. Such documents will help you prove that you're healthy and hence you won't contaminate the company's products.

You should never carry or chew gum while in the interview room. Even if you're worried that you might be having bad mouth odor, ensure that you've stopped chewing gum before entering the interview room. Chewing gum is an interview room is a sign of disrespect to the interviewers.

You should also ensure that your phone is switched off during the entire interview. What will happen if somebody calls you in the middle of the interview? Will you pick the phone, or ignore it? The interviewer might feel offended and disrespected if your phone starts ringing in the middle of the interview. A ringing phone can also easily distract you and hence confuse you when answering questions. This means that you'll be reducing chances of getting that job. Also remember to put your car keys in your pocket and not on the table inside the interview room.

Conclusion

In any interview you should never be in a hurry to answer any question. Take as much time as you can, to figure out the perfect answer. This way you'll minimize the probability of making errors and hence increase your chances of getting the job. However, you shouldn't take abnormally long periods of time before answering simple questions. If you do so, the interviewer can easily conclude that you're too slow and can't be able to do your job in time.

If you're so much interested in a given job, you must be willing to adapt to changes and lower your expectations. This basically means that you should always expect to do something more than your job description. If you've been given an assignment by your supervisor, you shouldn't be afraid or refuse to do it because it is not part of your job description.

At the end of the interview you should make it clear that it was an honor taking part in the interview and that you'll appreciate it if you get the job. You should also not walk out of the interview room without the interviewers go ahead. Wait until you've been cleared or ushered out of the room by the interviewer or his/her secretary.

So as to increase the probability of getting a job, you should try as much as possible to be the first or last person to be interviewed. Research shows that the first and last people in an interview are the most remembered. By simply being the first or last interviewee, you will significantly increase your chances of getting that job as the interviewer will remember you much, much more than the other candidates.

It is now up to you to start working on the tips listed in this book. With these tips, you can rest assured that you'll get that job that you've been dreaming of.

Good luck in your hunt for a job!!!

Author Bio

Colvin Tonya Nyakundi is a freelance writer and co-author of 'How to Get a Promotion at Work' Apart from that book, he has a portfolio of several other publications accumulated in the more than two years that he has been freelancing through www.odesk.com.

He has authored several personal relationships, construction and real estate, lifestyle and travel and holiday guide publications. Other books that he has co-authored include 'How to Survive in the Woods', 'How to Start Making Money Online', 'How to Survive in a Desert', 'How to Improve Your Communication Skills,' 'Construction Guide for New Investors in Real Estate,' 'How to Make Your Backyard a Magnificent Venue for Hosting Events', 'How to Identify the Perfect Holiday Destination', "How Your Favorite Meal Could be Killing You Slowly" and 'How to Prepare and Survive in a Foreign Country.' You can get in touch with him through his official Facebook account, tonyanc@facebook.com.

Check out some of the other JD-Biz Publishing books

Gardening Series on Amazon

Amazing Health Benefits of **Intermittent Fasting**	What Makes Me Fat?	**Natural Cures** of Anxiety	**Medical Conditions** Requiring **Paleo Diet**
Health Learning Series JD-Biz Publishing By M Usman and J Davidson	How to eliminate obesity naturally! Health Learning Series JD-Biz Publishing By M Usman and J Davidson	Health Learning Series JD-Biz Publishing By M Usman and J Davidson	Health Learning Series JD-Biz Publishing By M Usman and J Davidson
How to Eliminate Heart Burn and Acid Reflux Naturally	**Eliminate Pain!**	**Ways to Improve Self-Esteem**	**How to Avoid Brain Aging Dementia - Memory Loss Naturally**
Health Learning Series JD-Biz Publishing By M Usman and J Davidson	How to get rid of arthritis and joint pain naturally! Health Learning Series JD-Biz Publishing By M Usman and J Davidson	Health Learning Series JD-Biz Publishing By M Usman and J Davidson	Health Learning Series JD-Biz Publishing By M Usman and J Davidson
Paleo Diet Side Effects	**Paleo Diet** Good or Bad?	**How to Get Rid of High Blood Pressure or Hypertension Naturally**	**Health Benefits of Meditation**
Health Learning Series JD-Biz Publishing By M Usman and J Davidson	An Analysis of Arguments and Counter-Arguments Health Learning Series JD-Biz Publishing By M Usman and J Davidson	Health Learning Series JD-Biz Publishing By M Usman and J Davidson	Health Learning Series JD-Biz Publishing By M Usman and J Davidson
Paleo Diet For Weight Loss	**Paleo Diet** for Athletes	**How to Reduce the Chances of a Heart Attack**	**How to Get Rid of Asthma Naturally**
Health Learning Series JD-Biz Publishing By M Usman and J Davidson	Health Learning Series JD-Biz Publishing By M Usman and J Davidson	Health Learning Series JD-Biz Publishing By M Usman and J Davidson	Health Learning Series JD-Biz Publishing By M Usman and J Davidson

Amazing Animal Book Series

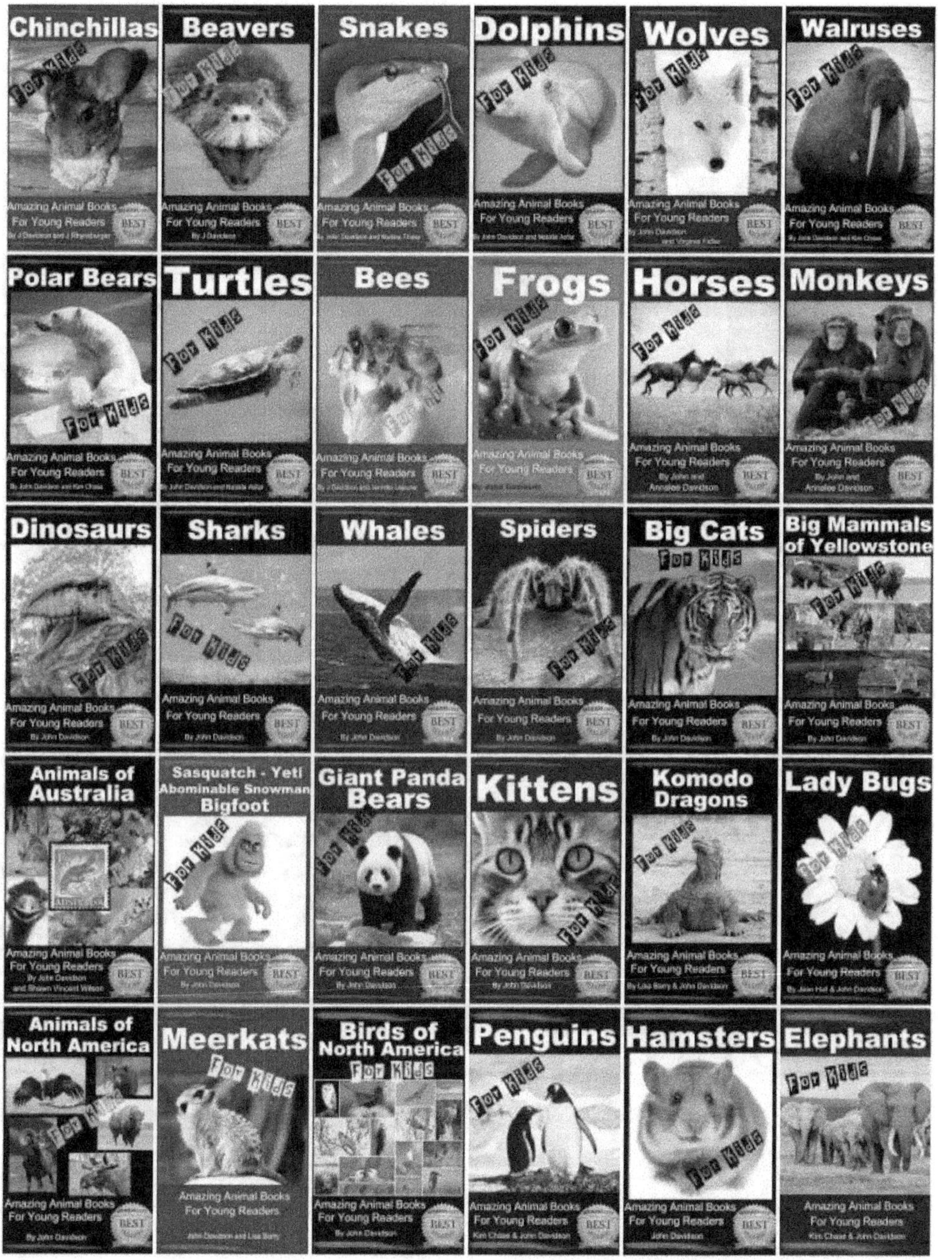

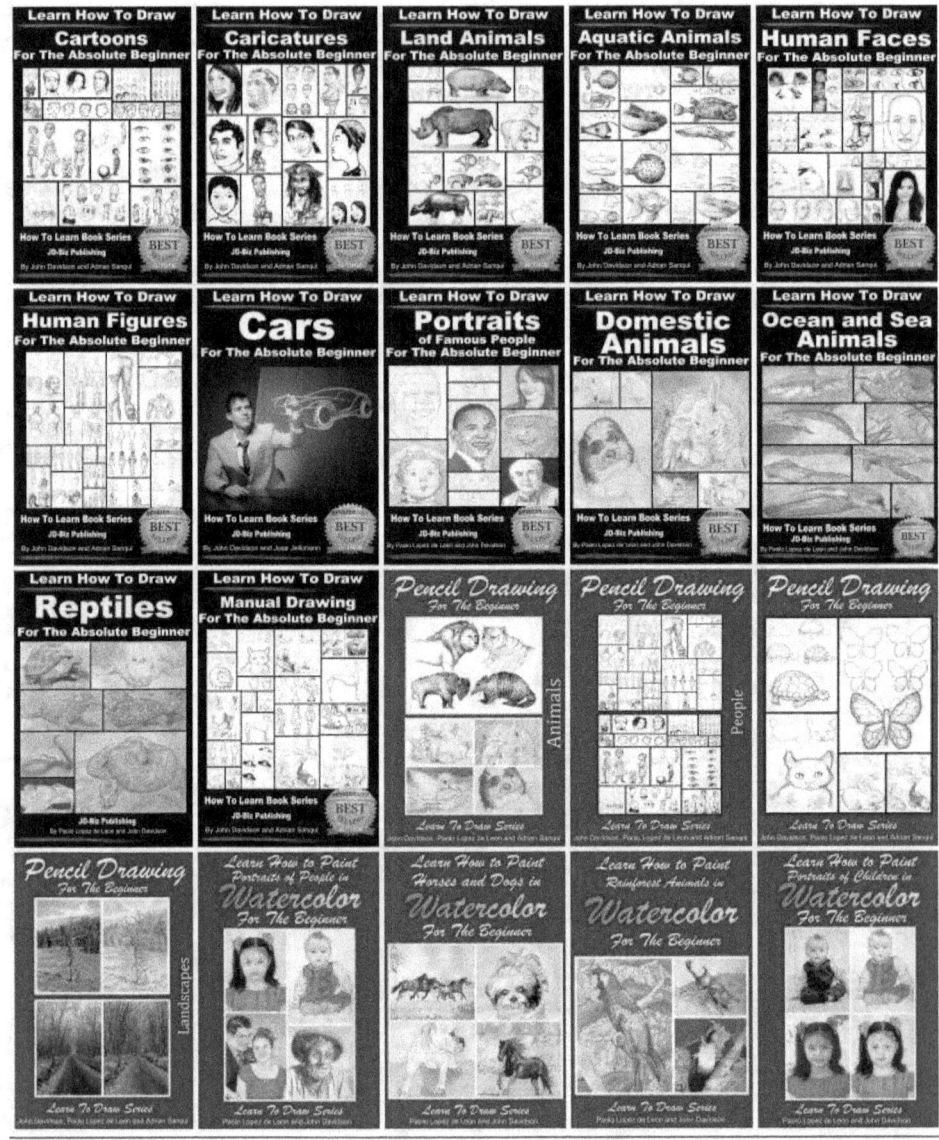

Entrepreneur Book Series

Our books are available at

1. Amazon.com

2. Barnes and Noble

3. Itunes

4. Kobo

5. Smashwords

6. Google Play Books

Publisher

JD-Biz Corp

P O Box 374

Mendon, Utah 84325

http://www.jd-biz.com/

Mendon Cottage Books

P O Box 374, Mendon Utah 84325

www.ingramcontent.com/pod-product-compliance
Lightning Source LLC
Chambersburg PA
CBHW072020290526
45787CB00013B/1520